D0354464

SPIKE LEE

better
The companion volume to the Universal Pictures film
Spike's own look at the people and events that made the film
TTER
ES
WITH LISA JONES
Do The Right Thing
SPIKE LEE

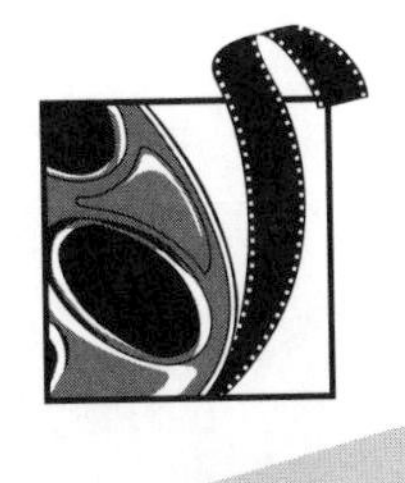

SPIKE LEE

On His Own Terms

by Melissa McDaniel

A Book Report Biography
FRANKLIN WATTS
A Division of Grolier Publishing
New York / London / Hong Kong / Sydney
Danbury, Connecticut

frontispiece: Spike Lee signs autographs and meets fans during a publicity tour.

Photographs ©: AP/Wide World Photos: 63 (Leita Cowart), 27, 60, 66; Archive Photos: 73; Beth Poppel Yearbook Archives: 24; Carol Kitman: 19; Corbis-Bettmann: 52; Gamma-Liaison: 22, 80 (Allen), 83 (Joe Wrinn); Globe Photos: 2 (Baret Lepejian), 56 (Bob Lucas), 13; New York Daily News: 75; New York University: 30; Photofest: 35, 48, 69, 78; Retna Pictures: cover (Gene Martin); Reuters/Archive Photos: 76 (Jeff Christiansen); The Kobal Collection: 17 (Lester Solan), 10, 33; 41, 46.

Visit Franklin Watts on the Internet at:
http://publishing.grolier.com

Library of Congress Cataloging-in-Publication Data
McDaniel, Melissa.
Spike Lee : on his own terms / by Melissa McDaniel.
p. cm.—(A book report biography)
Summary: Chronicles the life and career of controversial filmmaker Spike Lee.
Includes bibliographical references and index.
ISBN 0-531-11460-0 (lib. bdg.) 0-531-15935-3 (pbk.)
1. Lee, Spike—Juvenile literature. 2. Motion picture producers and directors—United States—Biography—Juvenile literature. 3. Afro-American motion picture producers and directors—United States—Biography. [1. Lee, Spike. 2. Motion picture producers and directors. 3. Afro-American motion picture producers and directors.] I. Title. II. Series.
PN1998.3.L44M33 1998
791.43'0233'092—dc21
[B] 98-10449
CIP
AC

Printed in the United States of America
1 2 3 4 5 6 7 8 9 10 R 07 06 05 04 03 02 01 00 99 98

CONTENTS

SPIKE LEE

CHAPTER ONE

SPIKE HAS IT

One Friday morning in 1986, an excited voice blared out over the airwaves, "You're going to want to be at the show tonight so you can tell your grandchildren in thirty years you were there." Spike Lee, a young black filmmaker, was announcing his arrival.

Spike's first feature film, *She's Gotta Have It*, was making its world premiere at the San Francisco Film Festival that evening. It told the story of Nola Darling, a bright young black woman juggling three boyfriends. All week Spike and his friends had been promoting the film, getting the word out, trying to build excitement. They wanted to sell the film to a distribution company during the festival. By Friday, Spike was confident. He was sure his film was going to blow the roof off the theater. On the way to the *screening*, he told a

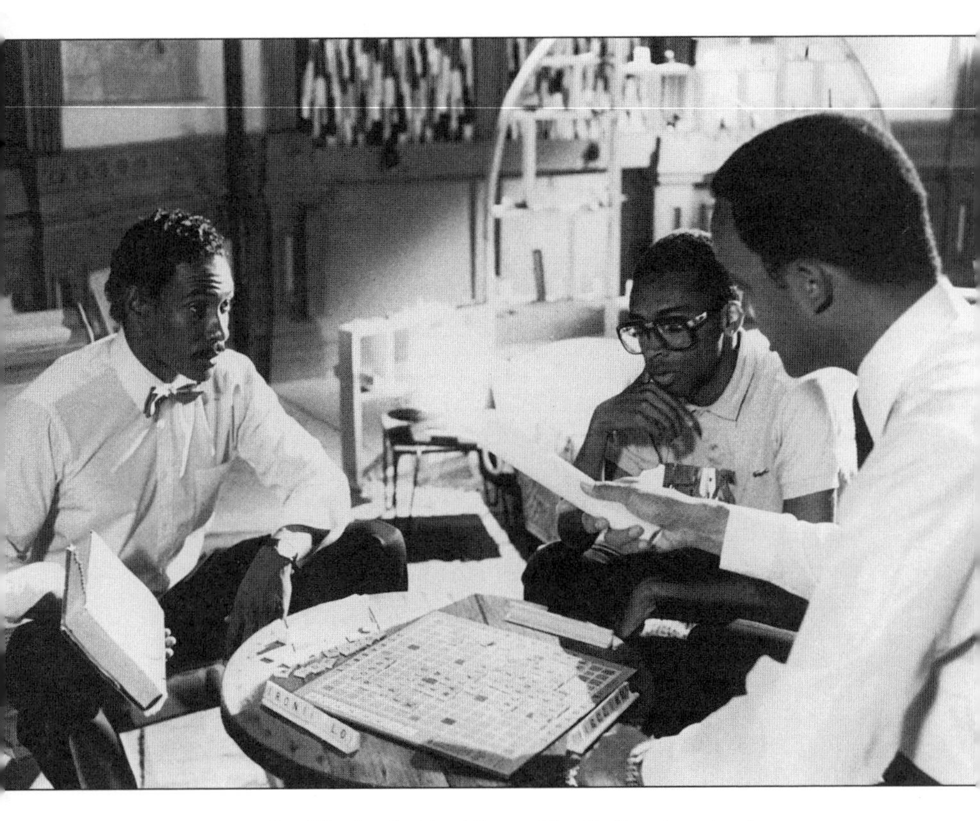

In She's Gotta Have It, *Spike (center) plays one of three men all chasing the same woman.*

friend, "I guess my life won't ever be the same after tonight."

As the lights in the Palace of Fine Arts Theater went down, a thousand people in the audience settled into their seats. Ten minutes into the film, one by one a dozen men looked straight into the camera and spoke the line they used to get a woman's interest. One man claimed, "You so fine baby, I'll drink a tub of your bathwater." The audience loved it, rocking with laughter and thoroughly enjoying themselves.

But almost twenty minutes later, the unbelievable happened. The house went dark. All across that San Francisco neighborhood, the electricity had gone out. Inside the theater, a thousand people who had been laughing just a minute earlier sat in total darkness. Even the emergency lights were out.

But nobody left. They all just sat in their seats, waiting to see the rest of the film. One person got up and stumbled through the darkness to where Spike and his friends were sitting. He was a film distributor named Ben Barenholtz. Although he had seen only a third of Spike's movie, he already knew he wanted to buy the rights to it. He had his checkbook out, ready to make a deal. This was no time to be negotiating, but clearly Spike's movie was a hot property.

The minutes passed. Finally, desperate to keep the audience in their seats, Spike got up on stage with a flashlight to answer questions. This went on for ten minutes before the police showed up to evacuate the theater. But no one in the crowd wanted to go. The officers began to get annoyed and were about to force people to leave when the lights flickered back on. Everyone in the audience cheered.

When the much-delayed film finally came to an end an hour later, the crowd sprang to their feet in a raucous standing ovation. They loved Spike and they loved his film.

Less than two months later, Spike dazzled another audience—this time in Cannes, France, at the world's most prestigious film festival. Once again, Lee received a standing ovation at the end of the film's screening.

When the film opened at a New York theater that August, lines formed around the block night after night. While many white people loved the movie, it was African-Americans who came out in droves. They sat in the theater, laughing and identifying with the characters. For the first time, many of them saw black characters on the big screen in romantic situations. "You never see black people kissing on the screen," Spike said. "Even the big stars, like Eddie Murphy and Richard Pryor, seem to be there just to make people laugh." He had

"Even the big stars, like Eddie Murphy and Richard Pryor, seem to be there just to make people laugh."

Spike has changed the way
African-Americans are portrayed on film.

changed that. Many African-Americans were relieved and proud to finally see themselves represented on screen as complex, if imperfect, people.

It was a magical time for Spike. Whenever he got the chance, he went down to the theater to sign and sell T-shirts promoting the film. *She's*

Gotta Have It eventually took in more than $8 million at the box office, making it one of the most successful *independent films* ever.

Brash, bold, and immensely talented, Spike Lee had immediately established himself as an important figure in American film. He knew he wanted to make provocative films that dealt with important issues among African-Americans. But he was also committed to making them great, entertaining movies. This was only the beginning.

CHAPTER TWO

A BROOKLYN CHILDHOOD

Shelton Jackson Lee came kicking and screaming into this world in Atlanta, Georgia, on March 20, 1957. Before he was even a year old, his mother had nicknamed him "Spike." "I guess she thought I was a tough baby," Lee once said.

Spike Lee traces his roots back to two Africans who were kidnapped and sold into slavery in America. "My great great great great grandfather Mike and his wife Phoebe were slaves," he explained. "They were broken up. Mike worked three or four years to buy his freedom and walked from South Carolina to Alabama to reunite with his wife and family. . . . That's my family. We've always been very strong, very proud, fearless, and intelligent."

Williams James Edwards, Spike Lee's great-grandfather, was the first descendant of Mike and Phoebe's to gain some fame. Edwards studied at the Tuskegee Institute, one of the nation's leading black colleges, which had been founded by Booker T. Washington. Edwards became a follower of Washington's and launched a career as an author and educator. In the 1890s, he founded the Snow Hill Institute in his hometown of Snow Hill, Alabama. It is now one of America's oldest black colleges.

Spike's father, Bill Lee, one of Edwards's grandchildren, attended Morehouse, a prestigious black college in Atlanta. There he met Jacqueline Shelton, a student at Spelman, Morehouse's sister college. The two married shortly after graduating.

Jackie Shelton also came from a proud family. In the 1930s in the United States, all the people depicted on birthday cards were white. But Jackie's mother, Zimmie Shelton, colored in the faces before she gave the cards to her friends and family. She also sought out black dolls for Jackie. She didn't want her daughter to think there was anything wrong with being black.

Spike's mother absorbed this pride in her heritage. She exposed her children to the work of great black writers like Zora Neale Hurston and Langston Hughes. She also fixed her hair in braids, in the African tradition, and she dressed in bold colors and prints long before these styles became popular.

Coming from such a proud and accomplished family had a powerful effect on Spike. It made him bold and confident. He grew up feeling that the world was his for the taking.

Spike is the eldest of Bill and Jackie Lee's four sons and one daughter. Bill Lee is a noted jazz bass player who has performed with such

Spike's strong family background has given him great confidence as a filmmaker.

musical legends as Billie Holiday and Duke Ellington. When Spike was still quite young, the family moved north to New York, where jazz music was popular and his father was more likely to find work.

For much of Spike's childhood, his family lived in a Brooklyn neighborhood called Cobble Hill, which was home mostly to working-class Italians, Puerto Ricans, and Jews. The Lees were the only black family around. Although Spike recalls being called "nigger" a couple of times when he first moved to Cobble Hill, mostly he remembers having a good time and playing sports with his neighbors.

Nothing mattered more to these Brooklyn kids. "We were all sports fanatics," Lee recalls fondly. "We played constantly, stopping only to eat, sleep, and argue about who was better, Yankees or Mets, Jets or Giants, Willie Mays or Mickey Mantle." Spike and his friends played everything—stickball, stoopball, basketball, football, punchball, softball. Although Spike was small and extremely quiet, he was always rounding people up for a game and he always put himself right in the center of the action. Spike was a natural-born leader.

"We were all sports fanatics"

Like these Brooklyn children, Spike spent much of his childhood playing basketball at the local playground.

He also followed the local teams closely. The New York Knicks were his favorite team. When the Mets made it to the World Series in 1969, his parents even let him miss three days of school to go to the games.

The young boy's world was also filled with art and culture. His parents wanted to expose him to everything. They took him to plays, films, and museums, instilling in him the importance of art.

Spike often accompanied his father to his *gigs* at jazz clubs and he would proudly tell people around him that the man onstage was his dad.

To Spike's father, jazz was the only music that mattered. While Spike liked jazz, he also liked rock 'n' roll, especially performed by such great Motown singers as the Temptations and the Supremes. Bill Lee hated pop music. He "didn't want that 'bad' music up in the house, so I had to listen to it at a very low volume or just wait till he wasn't around," Spike recalls.

Spike's mother was the family disciplinarian. She was the one who made the kids turn off the TV, do their homework, and go to bed at a reasonable hour. She pushed her children and expected great things from them. When Spike proudly showed her a report card with 85s in every subject, she said "That's good . . . but you have to do better next time. Get some 90s, like some of your white classmates. To be successful you have to be much better than they will be—not just as good. It's not fair, but that's the way it is."

"That's good . . . but you have to do better next time."

Their father was much more easygoing, sometimes too easygoing. He thought the children should be allowed to make their own decisions. Spike once joked that if he had said, "'Daddy, can we jump off the Brooklyn Bridge?' our father would say, 'Yeah, go 'head, have a good time!' and would stay hunched over his scattered sheets of music."

When Spike was about twelve, his family bought a brownstone in Fort Greene, a predominantly black, working-class neighborhood in Brooklyn. Although the Lees lived a middle-class life, money was sometimes scarce. Bill Lee was uncompromising. He believed in the purity of music, and when the electric bass became popular in jazz bands in the late 1960s, he refused to change with the times. He would not give up his large, upright bass with its rich, soulful sound. As a result, jobs were hard to come by. Spike's mother, an art and English teacher, often provided the family's only income. "We weren't starving but sometimes it was hand-to-mouth," Spike remembers. A few times, their electricity was turned off because they hadn't been able to pay the bill, and the Lees had to eat dinner by candlelight.

"We weren't starving but sometimes it was hand-to-mouth."

Spike Lee's father in 1990

Spike learned much from watching his father, who cared only about art and not at all about money. But talent alone wasn't enough to make him successful, and not having good money sense made it hard for him to take care of his family. Young Spike knew that if he was going to make it as an artist, he would have to be a businessman, too. "Having talent is not enough," Spike says. "You have to have some business know-how."

Jackie Lee taught at St. Ann's, a private school in Brooklyn Heights, a well-off, mostly white neighborhood. Some of the younger Lee children went to St. Ann's, but not Spike. Instead, he chose to go to John Dewey High School, an experimental public school with many black students. He didn't think it was right that his siblings should spend their teenage years in a mostly white environment. "It bothered me that they were in their formative years and didn't have any black friends," he once said. "Their socialization was almost totally white."

After graduating from high school in 1975, Lee followed the family tradition and, like his father and grandfather before him, went to Atlanta to attend all-black, all-male Morehouse College. His mother's mother, Zimmie Shelton, who lived in Atlanta, paid for his college education. She was not wealthy—she had been a teacher—but she saved all her money for her

Spike Lee hangs out with some friends in high school.

grandchildren. Throughout Spike's career, she came through for him, over and over again.

The year after Spike arrived at Morehouse, when he was just nineteen years old, his mother died of cancer. Spike recalls, "At the funeral, I felt I couldn't cry. I had to be the one to bow up. I was the eldest." Spike had always respected his mother, and as he grew older he came to realize what a tremendous influence she had been on him. "She inspired me to write," he says. "I got my drive from her."

"I got my drive from her."

Lee loved much about Morehouse. It was inspiring to live in a world where almost all the accomplished people around him were black. "Black professors, black doctors; it's a great experience in Atlanta," he later said.

Spike was not a great student, but he got involved in everything. He wrote for the school newspaper and had a jazz show on the campus radio station. His talent at rallying people around him also flourished. He later explained, "I was always the one to take the lead. When I went to Morehouse, there hadn't been an intramural softball team in ten years. I organized that. When you're a filmmaker, what you're really doing is motivating people. That's a gift I have." This was readily apparent when he took charge of directing the school's elaborate homecoming pageant in his senior year.

"I was always the one to take the lead."

It was at Morehouse that Spike first got involved with film. Although he had loved movies as a child, filmmaking had never jumped out at him as the one thing he wanted to do. But as a mass communications major, he began dabbling in film.

In 1977, between his sophomore and junior years, he bought a Super-8 movie camera and spent the summer shooting film. That summer there was a great blackout in New York. Electricity went out all over the city. Under cover of the darkness, many people broke into stores and stole whatever they could carry. Spike caught some of this on film. That summer was also the height of the disco-dancing craze, and the most popular dance was called the hustle. All around New York, people were out in the streets at block parties, dancing and enjoying themselves. Spike toted his camera around the city, shooting footage of people dancing.

He edited this footage into a documentary called *Last Hustle in Brooklyn*, which alternated between images of the blackout and the parties. The point of the movie was that people can hustle in more than one way. They can dance or they can do whatever it takes to get by, even if that means stealing. It was his first film, and it opened his eyes to the power of images.

By the time Spike graduated from Morehouse in 1979, he knew what he wanted to do with his life. Lee later wrote, "Film did something to me,

The 1977 blackout led to looting in several areas of New York City. This store owner looks over what's left of his merchandise the morning after the blackout.

for me, starting with looking through a viewfinder. I knew instinctively I had the vision for this line of work. I knew almost immediately that I would make films, and I knew that, once I made them, I didn't want hundreds of people to see them. I wanted millions of people to see them."

"I didn't want hundreds of people to see them. I wanted millions of people to see them."

CHAPTER THREE

SHAKE THEM UP

Spike Lee had grown up in an artistic family, and now he had found the art form that he would make his own. Unlike his father, he wouldn't be satisfied sitting alone at a piano composing music, or playing bass for a handful of people in a small club. Spike wanted people to notice. He wanted to "grab the people, shake them up—make them all pay attention." He would succeed almost immediately.

The summer after he graduated from college, Spike had an *internship* at Columbia Pictures in Los Angeles. Although he had considered going to film school in California, he decided that it wasn't for him. He didn't know enough people, and it would have cost a lot more than going to school in New York because he would have to pay for room and board. Besides, he didn't know how to drive. So that fall he headed back home to begin a three-year graduate film program at New York University.

New York University has one of the most renowned and competitive film schools in the country. When Spike arrived there, only a few other black students were enrolled in the film program. He got himself noticed almost immediately.

New York University surrounds Washington Square Park in Manhattan.

During his first year, he made a ten-minute film called *The Answer*. It tells the story of a black screenwriter who is given the job of doing a remake of *The Birth of a Nation*, a silent film made in 1915 by director D. W. Griffith, who is often called "the father of American cinema." *The Birth of a Nation* glorifies the actions of the violent racist group known as the Ku Klux Klan, while depicting blacks as dangerous and animalistic. It is nonetheless considered a classic because of Griffith's innovative filmmaking techniques. More than two hours long, it was the first epic film, and Griffith's use of close-ups and cutaways gave it unprecedented emotional power. But to Spike, the film's importance in the development of cinema did not make up for its racism.

He knew that as a first-year film student, taking on a giant of cinema would cause some controversy. But he didn't care. "I knew they wouldn't like it," he said. He was right. Some of his professors questioned the film's merit. "The attitude was, 'How dare I denigrate the father of cinema, D. W. Griffith!'" Already Lee had served notice that he would be more than happy to make some waves any time they needed to be made.

The remainder of his time at film school was smoother. In his second year, he won a teaching assistantship that paid his *tuition*, which allowed him to put the money that his grandmother had given him for tuition into making films. That year he made *Sarah*, the story of a family gathering in Harlem on Thanksgiving.

Lee wanted to make films that realistically explored the black experience, something that had almost never happened on film. In the aftermath of *The Birth of a Nation*, some blacks had begun making movies for themselves to avoid racist stereotypes. This was the beginning of "race movies," films made by, for, and about blacks. Directors such as Oscar Micheaux made dramas, comedies, romances, and mysteries—films in every genre. Black actors finally had the opportunity to play detectives and sex symbols and crooks—the full range of roles that had always been open to whites. By the 1950s, however, race movies had died out.

In Hollywood, meanwhile, blacks were not faring so well. Almost all their roles were either comic or dangerous characters. Then, in the 1960s, Sidney Poitier became the first black movie star. He never played the degrading parts that blacks were traditionally given. Instead, his characters were almost too perfect. They were always doctors, policemen, scientists, and other well-educated professionals. While this was a welcome improvement, these idealized characters were not fully rounded, realistic human beings. They often seemed intended to show whites that blacks could be as good as them.

Sidney Poitier was the first black actor in Hollywood to play roles that were not stereotypes. However, his characters frequently seemed to have no troubles at all.

In 1971, African-American director Melvin Van Peebles made *Sweet Sweetback's Baadasssss Song*, the story of a black man in the ghetto being pursued by the police. Black audiences cheered Sweetback's exploits. This film inspired Hollywood to begin producing what became known as "blaxploitation" films, with violent, jive-talking heros. But audiences soon tired of these films.

Two black filmmakers had succeeded in making warm, subtle, and insightful films about black life. But neither Gordon Parks's *The Learning Tree* nor Charles Burnett's *The Killer of Sheep* reached huge audiences, and the directors had been unable to get funding to make films on a regular basis.

Spike Lee didn't want to be banished to the art houses. He wanted to make serious—and seriously fun—pictures that would put bodies in the seats.

Lee's last film at NYU, *Joe's Bed-Stuy Barbershop: We Cut Heads* was an honest and humorous look at a barbershop that fronts for a gambling ring in the black Brooklyn neighborhood of Bedford-Stuyvesant. The film's lead character must choose between making some quick money in the illegal numbers racket or staying clear of it.

Like many of Spike's films, this one was made with the help of his friends and family. His grand-

In Joe's Bed-Stuy Barbershop: We Cut Heads, *Spike avoided traditional stereotypes of African-Americans.*

mother supplied the money for it. His father composed the music. Ernest Dickerson, one of the few other black students at the NYU film school, was the film's *cinematographer.* And a good friend from Morehouse—Monty Ross—starred in the film.

Although Spike had just graduated from film school, his talent was already turning heads. *Joe's Bed-Stuy Barbershop: We Cut Heads* won a student Academy Award from the Academy of Motion Picture Arts and Sciences and was the first student film ever shown in the prestigious New Directors/New Films series in New York City. Spike Lee was on his way.

Winning such impressive honors drew the attention of such leading talent agencies as ICM and William Morris, but he didn't get any work. Spike later said that the experience "cemented in my mind what I always thought all along: that I would have to go out and do it alone, not rely on anyone else." If Hollywood wouldn't give him work, then he'd make a movie independently.

"I would have to go out and do it alone, not rely on anyone else."

He wrote a script called *The Messenger* about a New York City bike messenger. Lee had hired a cast and crew and had been preparing for the shoot for two months when it became apparent that he didn't have enough money to make the film. The project was dead before the film had even begun to roll. But a lot of money had already been spent.

"In total, we lost about fifty grand," he recalls. "I couldn't sleep at night. I couldn't eat because I would throw up. . . . Folks were mad as hell." Lee was devastated and frustrated. One night, he took to his bathtub for consolation. "I must have sat in that tub and cried for an hour," he said. "I was wrinkled as a raisin when I got out."

"I couldn't sleep at night. I couldn't eat because I would throw up. . . . Folks were mad as hell."

But when he got out, he knew what he needed to do. He needed to start over again. This time, however, he would pick a project that could be made for much less money but would still appeal to a lot of people. He later explained, "I needed to do a movie that would have very few characters and needed next to no location work, sets, or costumes."

The answer soon came to him, and during the next few months he wrote *She's Gotta Have It*. The film could be made cheaply because most of it takes place in one apartment and a nearby park. And since most of it is conversation, it required no tricky shots that would be expensive to film.

Still, Spike had trouble coming up with the money. At the beginning of the shoot, he had little more than an $18,000 grant from the New York State Council on the Arts. Throughout the shoot, he asked everybody he knew for whatever money they could spare. "We never knew where the next nickel was going to come from," Lee recalls, "so we wrote to or called everybody we knew in the world, asking them to send money, even if it was just $50. Each day, while we were shooting, someone would go back to my house to see if any checks had come."

Spike had been able to shoot the film in just twelve days, but he was still going to need a lot of time and money to put it all together. "If I don't raise some money, I'll be selling tube socks on Fourteenth street," he said. He screened the unfinished film before a group of black businesspeople, hoping that some of them would be willing to invest in the film. But he had no luck. They weren't willing to put money into his odd black-and-white project. Eventually, with checks from a couple of people and favors from friends in the industry, he was able to complete the film. His total budget was just $175,000.

In the film, Lee plays Mars Blackmon, one of the three men in Nola Darling's life. Mars is a skinny little hip-hop homeboy with giant square glasses and a huge gold necklace in the shape of his name. Nola likes him because he makes her laugh. After the success of the film, people often expected Spike to be like Mars. "Lots of people are disappointed when they meet me. . . . I'm quiet and reserved and they expect me to be a ranting, raving lunatic."

"Lots of people are disappointed when they meet me. . . . I'm quiet and reserved."

While Spike was not always ranting and raving, he was more than willing to speak his mind on virtually any topic. Even before *She's Gotta Have It* had premiered, he had blasted star Whoopi Goldberg for wearing blue contact lenses, which to Spike means that she wants to be white. Soon he took on other major players as well. He criticized pop legend Michael Jackson for altering his appearance to make himself look whiter and white director Steven Spielberg for directing *The Color Purple*, a movie about black people.

Spike seemed to be everywhere. He appeared on the *Today* show and *Saturday Night Live*, directed a music video for jazz legend Miles Davis, and his picture was on the cover of *Jet* magazine. In less than a year, he was making commercials for Nike and appearing as Mars Blackmon alongside one of his idols—basketball superstar Michael Jordan.

She's Gotta Have It eventually earned more than $8 million at the box office, demolishing the Hollywood idea that black films don't sell. "The whole point is that you can take an unknown, all-black cast and put them in a story that comes from black experience, and all kinds of people will come to see it if it's a good film," Lee explains. "I wish Hollywood would get that message."

With his second film, Lee was sending a different message to a different group of people. He resurrected an old script he had written called *Homecoming*, about life at a black college, and renamed it *School Daze*. He was ready to make trouble and enjoy doing it. "This film is going to cause havoc," he said with a laugh before the film came out. "People are going to say, 'Spike, why bring this out? Why let white people know about this? We need to move on. And there are just some things that should be kept in the family.' "

"People are going to say, 'Spike, why bring this out?' "

The film takes place on an all-black campus closely resembling Morehouse, where Lee went to college. Never before had a film taken on such touchy issues among African-Americans as divisions based on skin tone. The students in the film break into *cliques* based upon their skin color. The

In this musical scene from School Daze, *two groups of black women mock the other's skin color and hairstyles.*

dark-skinned students with kinky hair are called Jigaboos. Most of them are the first in their family to go to college. The lighter-skinned students with straight hair are more affluent and are considered more beautiful. They are called Wannabes, because they "wannabe" white.

Lee also confronted the hostility between the politically active students and those who just want to slide into a good job on Wall Street. He dealt with conflicts between the middle-class students and the poor kids from the surrounding neighborhoods. "What I tried to do with this film is point out what I feel are all the superficial and petty differences that keep black people apart," Spike explained. The film ends with one character screaming "Wake up" over and over again. It was a call for black people to take pride in themselves and for the black community to overcome these internal conflicts.

Lee went to Atlanta to shoot the film. In the middle of filming on the Morehouse campus, the school administration realized what the movie was about and decided that it would reflect badly on the school. They kicked Spike off the campus. He took this rejection in stride and simply moved the production to Atlanta University.

These strong reactions continued after the film was completed. The United Negro College Fund canceled plans for a benefit premiere because of the film's subject. When Spike went on the *Today* show to promote the film, Bryant Gumbel, the show's African-American host, was highly critical of Spike making a film about these sorts of problems within the black community. Gumbel didn't show a clip from the film or say when it was opening. He was completely hostile. Reportedly, he later tried to call Lee and apologize.

Spike was also having trouble with his studio, Columbia Pictures. By the time the film was complete, David Puttnam, the Columbia executive who had enthusiastically supported the picture, had been replaced by Dawn Steel, who didn't care about any of Puttnam's films. Because she wasn't interested in the movie, the studio didn't do much to promote it. Lee was incensed when he learned that the studio was not going to do any television commercials or put any advertisements in black magazines such as *Jet, Essence*, or *Ebony*. To Lee, it was insulting: the studio wasn't willing to put money behind the project because it was a black film.

The film opened to mixed reviews. Some people said it was messy. Others complained that its tone was wildly inconsistent. This reaction was partly because it was a musical. Some people felt it was just too strange to be dealing with serious social issues in song. And many viewers objected that the female characters had too little to do. While the male characters were arguing about political issues, the females were just arguing about guys.

But none of this kept the film from being a success. *School Daze* cost $6 million, got mixed reviews, and still made $14 million. Once again, Lee had proved that if you put interesting black characters on the screen, people will fill the seats.

CHAPTER FOUR

DOING THE RIGHT THING

"Controversial or political subject matter can work well at the box office," Spike Lee once said. If newspapers and radio programs are debating a film, praising it or condemning it, that's a lot of free publicity, and more people are likely to go see the movie. "I'm used to getting out there and pushing my films in any way I can," Spike says. "[I] try to make thought-provoking films that are entertaining. It's a hard juggling act, balancing what is good business and good art, but it can be done."

He proved just how good he was at this with his next film, *Do the Right Thing* (1989). This time Lee found himself at the center of the public debate about race in America. Spike didn't want to make a somber movie about racism. Instead, his film is exuberant and explosive, fast and funny, filled with bright colors and bold compositions.

Do the Right Thing takes place on one Brooklyn block in Bedford-Stuyvesant, a black community, on the hottest day of the summer. When the mercury goes up, people get more irritable. Lee wanted to show how the heat can make racial tensions come to the surface.

Do the Right Thing *takes place on a scorching hot day, when many people in the neighborhood are sitting outside to escape the heat.*

The heat has pushed all the people in the neighborhood outside, where they are trying to get some air and catch a little bit of breeze. They hang out on the stoops and sidewalks, watching and commenting on the day's events.

Spike plays Mookie, the film's main character. Money is always on Mookie's mind, mainly because it is in short supply. He's often been without a job, but now he's working as a pizza deliveryman. Although he has a son that his girlfriend is raising, Mookie lives with his sister. Both women are tired of him being irresponsible.

Mookie works at Sal's Famous Pizzeria, the only white business left on the block. Sal is a friendly guy who runs the place with the help of his sons, Vito and Pino. While Vito is a nice, quiet kid, Pino is a rabid racist who resents having to sweat all day making food for black people.

As the day goes on and the temperature rises, tensions build and tempers flare. While buying a slice of pizza, Buggin' Out, an excitable guy with giant eyes, notices that Sal has pictures of famous Italians, such as Frank Sinatra and Al Pacino, on the wall of the pizzeria. But there are no pictures of black people. He asks Sal why. Sal answers that it's his pizzeria, so he can put whomever he wants on the wall. If Buggin' Out wants pictures of African-Americans on the wall, he should open his own place.

In this scene from Do the Right Thing, *Sal (left) argues with Buggin' Out (sitting to the right).*

Buggin' Out is furious, and he tries to rouse the other people in the neighborhood to boycott Sal's. That evening, he and Radio Raheem, a huge man with an equally huge boom box, return to the pizzeria. They demand that some blacks be put on the wall. Radio Raheem turns the volume on his radio way up. Sal explodes, calls him a "nigger," and smashes the boom box. They get into a fight, which spills out into the street. When the police show up, they use a choke hold on Radio Raheem. By the time they let go, he is dead.

Mookie is outraged. He throws a garbage can through the window of Sal's, starting a riot. The pizzeria burns to the ground.

The film ends with two quotes. One, by Martin Luther King Jr., includes the statement, "Violence as a way of achieving racial justice is both impractical and immoral." The other, by Malcolm X, concludes, "I am not against using violence in self-defense. I don't even call it violence when it is self-defense, I call it intelligence."

Nobody in the film is perfect. Lee is affectionate toward all the neighborhood characters. But he also pokes fun at Radio Raheem's gigantic boom box, at Buggin' Out freaking out when somebody accidentally steps on his new Air Jordans, and at Mookie's irresponsibility. And Sal, who thinks of himself as *liberal*, uses the word "nigger" when push comes to shove. "There are no heroes," says Lee.

"There are no heroes."

If Spike wanted to get some free publicity, he had succeeded. Some people said the film would provoke riots. In *Newsweek* magazine, Jack

Kroll wrote that it is "dynamite under every seat." *New York* magazine's Joe Klein called it a "reckless" movie with a "dangerously stupid" message. He said that it taught black teenagers that whites are the enemy. "It's racist to assume black people can't distinguish between what's real and what's on the screen," Lee shot back with exasperation. "This is not a dangerous movie. But what frightens people is that what's in the movie is reality."

Lee and Klein went on the *Oprah Winfrey* show to talk about the film. Klein's alarmism didn't go over well with Oprah's audience. In the *Amsterdam News*, Abiola Sinclair, a black writer who had never been a big fan of Spike's, reported that Klein "was trying to defend his position amid guffaws and pooh-poohs from the largely white audience. He looked like the jerk he is."

The film focused America's attention on racism as no movie had in a long time. "I think it is really hard for white America to understand what it means to be black," Lee says. "Every day you're faced with racism. If you're black, you have been called 'nigger' more than once and it becomes a part of your life." Over and over again, reporters asked Lee how Mookie could

"I think it is really hard for white America to understand what it means to be black."

destroy a place where he worked. But no one ever asked about Radio Raheem's death. To Lee, this meant that white-owned property meant more to them than a black person's life. "Mookie did what he did because he was angry," Lee said. "He saw for himself how the system destroys black people."

Many people, black and white, saw the film for what it was—a brilliant piece of filmmaking and one of the best movies of the decade. In *Newsweek*, David Ansen commented, "You leave the movie stunned, challenged, drained. . . . It's the funkiest and most informed view of racism an American filmmaker has given us." Critic Roger Ebert, of the *Chicago Sun-Times*, reminded viewers of what a fun and funny movie it was, calling the film "an entertaining, upbeat, joyous slice of life." Many reviewers put it on their year's "ten best" list.

The following spring, Lee was nominated for an Academy Award® for Best Original Screenplay. He was the first African-American ever nominated in that category. But the film was not among the five nominees for Best Picture. During the Oscars ceremony, actress Kim Basinger got up to introduce a film clip. But first she said, "We have five great films here and they are great for one reason: they tell the truth. But there is one film missing from the list that deserves to be honored because, ironically, it might tell the biggest truth

At the Academy Awards, Kim Basinger tells the audience that Spike's movie should have been nominated for Best Picture.

of all. And that's *Do the Right Thing."* Many people in the audience burst into applause. Spike was surprised and grateful and sent Basinger a thank-you note after she sat down.

For his next film, Spike turned his attention to a more personal subject—jazz. He felt that no movie had ever done justice to the music itself. Too often, movies had either focused on white performers or reveled in the musicians' personal problems.

He wanted to do something different. "We didn't want it raining in every scene. We didn't want dark and gloom and doom and smoke and pathos and drugs and alcohol. And no humor. We wanted people to see these guys rehearsing and composing, perfecting their craft," he said. He would show musicians creating music and depict the culture that fuels jazz. And he would bathe the whole film with a moody, jazzy feel.

Bleek Gilliam, the main character in *Mo' Better Blues* (1990), is carrying on relationships with two women at the same time. He is emotionally distant from both, always telling them that his trumpet comes first.

Some African-Americans have argued that Spike's imperfect characters are not realistic. "I think it's a trap every black artist is faced with," he says. "Anytime you do a role or write a novel where some black people aren't 100 percent angelic, people want to scream that you're holding the race back. I try not to get into that debate. I think it would be very boring dramatically to have a film where everybody was a lawyer or doctor and had no faults, no nothing. To me, the most important thing is to be truthful." But in *Mo' Better Blues*, both of Bleek's smart, accomplished girlfriends know about each other. Some people questioned whether, in the real world, the women would put up with Bleek.

"To me, the most important thing is to be truthful."

With his next film, Spike returned to subject matter guaranteed to stir up debate. *Jungle Fever* (1991) concerned a romance between a black architect and an Italian-American secretary from his office. The film got many people talking about the issue of interracial romance and whether blacks are betraying their community by dating whites. But while the movie did well at the box office, it did not generate the kind of excitement that *Do the Right Thing* had. To a certain extent, *Jungle Fever* was overshadowed by Spike's next project, which he was already working on. This would be a film that would throw him into the headlines again and again.

CHAPTER FIVE

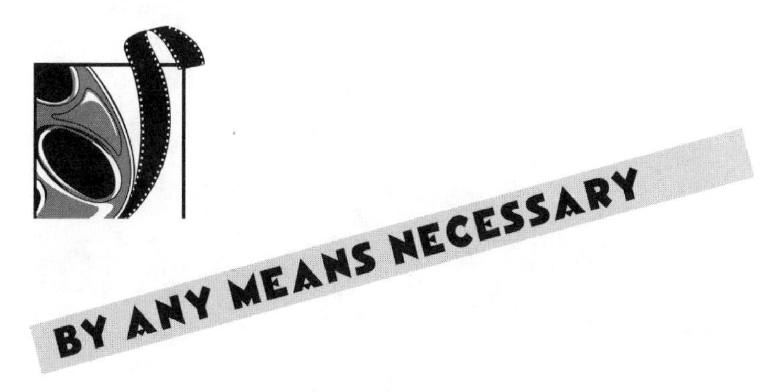

BY ANY MEANS NECESSARY

"I hate and refuse to lose," Spike once wrote. Nowhere is this more obvious than in his struggle to bring the life of black nationalist leader Malcolm X to the screen. Many people had wanted to film Malcolm's story, the saga of a man who was constantly growing, learning, and evolving throughout his life.

Malcolm Little was born in Omaha, Nebraska. As a young man in Boston and New York, he became involved in crime and drugs, and he went to jail for burglary. There he discovered the teachings of Elijah Muhammad, the leader of the Nation of Islam, who advocated black separatism and self-reliance. He instructed his followers to live a strict moral lifestyle, not indulging in drugs or alcohol. He also taught that white people were evil.

With Elijah Muhammad's encouragement, Malcolm dropped the name Little, because it had

Malcolm X (standing in front of the microphone) addresses a crowd in Harlem, New York City. A legendary speaker, Malcolm X became one of the most controversial African-American leaders of the 1950s and 1960s.

been given to his enslaved ancestors by their white masters, and began calling himself Malcolm X, which symbolized his unknown African family name. A powerful speaker, he became the Nation of Islam's leading spokesman and mesmerized listeners with his call for black unity and self-sufficiency. Blacks would achieve their rights, he said, "by any means necessary."

Gradually, Malcolm fell out of favor with the Nation of Islam. He learned that Elijah Muhammad had fathered children by many different young women, and he became disillusioned with the old man's hypocrisy. In 1964, Malcolm made a *pilgrimage* to Mecca, Saudi Arabia, the holy city of Islam, where he discovered that many of Elijah Muhammad's teachings had little to do with traditional Islam. This trip was a deeply spiritual experience for Malcolm. It also changed his attitude toward white people. He told the press, "During the past 11 days here in the Muslim world, I have eaten from the same plate, drank from the same glass, and slept in the same bed while praying to the same God with fellow-Muslims, whose eyes were the bluest of blue, whose hair was the blondest of blond, and whose skin was the whitest of white." Although Malcolm now rejected all racism, he never renounced the principle of black self-reliance.

In 1965, Malcolm was gunned down by members of the Nation of Islam at the Audubon Ballroom in Harlem. He was just 39 years old when he was murdered.

People had been trying to film a story about the life of Malcolm X since 1969, when producer Marvin Worth bought the rights to *The Autobiography of Malcolm X* from Malcolm's widow, Betty Shabazz, and the writer Alex Haley, who had collaborated with Malcolm on the book. Worth hired the great African-American writer James Baldwin and an experienced screenwriter named Arnold Perl to work on an adaptation of Malcolm's autobiography.

They were never quite able to get it right, however, nor did the eminent writers such as David Bradley and David Mamet who tackled it over the years. Directors such as Sidney Lumet and Bob Fosse and actors such as Richard Pryor had also shown interest in the project, but no one had been able to make it come together.

Then, in 1990, Worth finally thought he had a team that could make it work. Charles Fuller, a prominent black playwright, had agreed to write the screenplay. Denzel Washington would play Malcolm. And the director would be Norman Jewison, an accomplished white filmmaker who had made several well-received movies that dealt with racial themes. In 1983, all three men had worked together on *A Soldier's Story*, a drama about racial tensions on an army base. Jewison was probably most famous for his 1967 film *In the Heat of the Night*, a powerful drama about a northern policeman, played by Sidney Poitier, who becomes involved in a murder investigation in a southern town. Worth was happy with the talent he had brought together. It seemed that finally, after more than a decade of effort, the life of Malcolm X would make it to the big screen.

But then Spike got into the act. He started complaining to the media about a white man directing the life story of such an important black figure. "I have a big problem with Norman Jewison directing *The Autobiography of Malcolm X*," he said. "That disturbs me deeply. It's wrong with a capital W. Blacks have to control these films. Malcolm X is one of our most treasured heroes. To let a non-African-American do it is a travesty."

"It's wrong with a capital W. Blacks have to control these films."

Spike had brought up a very thorny issue. Many writers and filmmakers began debating the subject. Malcolm's life "is the story of a man who learns to transcend race," said David Bradley, a black novelist who had earlier taken a stab at the screenplay. "It's a stupid notion that there's a

Norman Jewison, who was going to direct a film about Malcolm X, became the target of Spike's criticism.

black aesthetic, a black experience. Malcolm never was a Christian—does that mean you have to have a black Muslim director?"

But Spike was adamant that his experience as an African-American enabled him to bring extra nuance and understanding to the story. He explained that he was "not saying that only Chinese people can direct Chinese films, that only black people can direct black films, or that only white people can direct white films. I don't think it should be that way, but there are specific cases where because of your background, because you know the subject matter, it enhances your work. This film needed someone who doesn't have to read a book to know what it is to be called a 'nigger' in this country."

Worth eventually called Lee and asked him to stop complaining about Jewison in the press. The two men started talking about the possibility of Lee directing the film. Meanwhile, Jewison was having trouble getting a script he was satisfied with. Finally, he said, "I don't know how to do this film, I can't lick it." He wished Lee well, and that was that. The movie was Spike's to make.

But that would not be easy. First, Spike had to come up with a script that he liked. He went back and read all those that had been attempted previously. The best by far, he thought, was the original one written by Baldwin and Perl. Spike started revising it, filling in some holes. He eventually came up with a version that satisfied him.

Meanwhile, he and Warner Brothers, the studio producing the film, were arguing over the budget. Spike had figured out that it would cost $33 million to do the film right; Warner Brothers would put up only $26 million. Spike decided to go ahead with it anyway. He didn't want it to be another twenty years until the film was made. He told himself, "Hell, no! No delays over money-haggling. We're going to shoot this film by hook or crook. By any means necessary."

Not everyone was happy that Spike Lee was making a movie about Malcolm X. The loudest objections came from an African-American Muslim named Amiri Baraka, who is an eminent poet and social critic. Baraka argued that Lee's earlier films had shown little understanding of black Muslims or concern for the struggle of poor blacks. Baraka was concerned that Lee would emphasize the parts of Malcolm's life that were natural for a movie, such as his days as a criminal. Lee blasted back, "I'm gonna make the kind of film I want to make. . . . And who appointed Baraka chairman of the African-American arts committee? Nobody

"I'm gonna make the kind of film I want to make."

tells him what poems and plays to write, so why is he trying to tell me what kind of film to make?"

Once Spike began filming, he kept running into trouble. Betty Shabazz had been asking to see the script for a long time, and he finally showed it to her. She hated it. She objected to scenes in which she and Malcolm argued. "She

Malcolm X's wife, Betty Shabazz, complained to Spike about a scene in which she and Malcolm argue.

came and told me she and Malcolm never fought. Now what married couple in the history of the world has never had an argument?" Spike wondered. Meanwhile, Spike's girlfriend, Veronica Webb, a model who had a small part in the film, dumped him. While he was still reeling from this, more serious trouble arose—his father was arrested for possession of heroin. "He'd been doing that for years. Not shooting but snorting," Lee later said. Although his father had been arrested two or three times previously, the news had never been made public. But this time, Lee says, "When they caught him, he said, 'I'm Spike Lee's father! Spike's my son!' He sacrificed me just to avoid spending a night in jail."

Spike knew that news of his father's arrest would be splattered all across the front page of the New York *tabloids* the next day. "I really dreaded going in for the next morning's shoot," he recalled. The film's cast and crew tried to protect him. That was the only day he did not see a single newspaper on the set.

Then a young woman who was an extra in the film was found murdered in her apartment. Although the crime was in no way related to the film, it again made tabloid headlines.

For Spike, it seemed like there had been an endless stream of bad publicity and headaches, just one thing after another. "Sometimes it was hard to concentrate on directing during this time," Spike has said. "But I had to do it because nobody is going to sit out in the audience and say, 'Well, cousin, it's a [lousy] movie true enough, but the brother was going through some hard times . . . and we should cut him some slack."

By the time Lee had finished shooting the film, it was already way over budget, and it hadn't even been edited yet. When the studio refused to give him any more money, Spike decided to get the money himself. "Malcolm always preached self-reliance," he later reflected. "I didn't have to sit around begging the studio to give me anything." Instead, he turned to some of the most prominent African-Americans in the country. Bill Cosby, Michael Jordan, Oprah Winfrey, Janet Jackson, and Tracy Chapman all contributed cash to keep the production moving. The studio eventually kicked in some money to finish the film.

By the time the film was actually released, *Malcolm X* had already been on everyone's mind for two years. Before Spike had even completed *Jungle Fever*, he had come up with a design for a hat promoting *Malcolm X*. It was simple—a silver X on a baseball cap. He wanted to get the thought out there, start the excitement. Spike had always sold T-shirts and other goods promoting his films,

Spike wears his 'X' hat to promote Malcolm X.

but nothing had ever taken off like the X hat. They were everywhere. And Spike hadn't even started working on the film yet.

But Malcolm was much more than a hat. As the film's premiere approached, everyone was talking and arguing about Malcolm X's life and message. He meant very different things to different people, and people wondered: which Malcolm would Spike Lee put on the screen?

Spike wanted to grab people's attention from the first moment of the film. The movie begins with an American flag that bursts into flames and burns down into an X. Intercut with this are images of a black motorist named Rodney King being beaten by white policemen in Los Angeles. The film ends with scenes shot in South Africa, where whites brutally oppressed blacks for centuries. Spike was sending a message: Malcolm X is as relevant today as he was in the 1960s.

The film itself is a big, bold epic in classic Hollywood style. Early on, Malcolm and his friend Shorty, played by Lee, roam around in loud suits. There is even an elaborate musical number in a dance hall. Then the film settles down to seriousness as Lee follows Malcolm's journey.

Spike says that in the film he wanted to stress the importance Malcolm placed on education, "Because our value system has been twisted around so that it's not uncommon for young black kids who are smart, who are intelligent, who speak good English, who receive As in school, to be ridiculed by other black kids for being 'white.' I think that's really crazy. A lot of kids fail classes and get bad grades on purpose so they won't be ridiculed by their friends." For Malcolm, there was no greater insult than to say, "That's not intelligent."

No film in recent memory had been more anticipated. In many ways, it was impossible for the film to live up to all the hype. Most critics liked and respected the film but were not excited by it. Instead of Lee's usual flair and originality, they saw a conventional Hollywood biography. "It's done with impressive skill and style," wrote David Sterritt in the *Christian Science Monitor*, "but it's hardly the explosive experience" that people had anticipated.

Denzel Washington was singled out for praise again and again. Everyone agreed that he had brought Malcolm to life. David Sterritt said Washington gave an "extraordinary performance" that "is never less than riveting." Washington was named the year's best actor by the New York Film Critic's Circle and earned an Oscar nomination.

The film eventually earned $48 million at the box office, but many people had hoped for and expected more. Some observers concluded that

Denzel Washington (right), who won acclaim for his portrayal of Malcolm, with Spike, who plays Malcolm's friend Shorty

after hearing so much about Malcolm for so long, Americans were simply tired of it.

Still, Spike Lee had made history. *Malcolm X* had the highest budget of any movie with a black director. He had made the first African-American epic, and he had done it on his own terms.

When all was said and done, he was proud and ecstatic about what he had accomplished. "It's the best thing I've ever done," he exclaimed. "Again and again this film will be shown . . . introduced to a new generation of people every year. It is the success I expected."

"It's the best thing I've ever done."

CHAPTER SIX

FROM CROOKLYN TO THE WORLD

In a way, everything in Spike Lee's career had been leading up to *Malcolm X*. But once it was done, it was not obvious what he should do next.

The one thing Spike knew was that he needed a break. "I needed a chance to regroup. I really wanted to chill out a bit," he said. Little was seen of him until October 1993, when he married a lawyer named Tonya Lewis after a year-long romance. The couple now have two children, a daughter, Satchel, and a son, Jackson.

Family was also the focus of his next film. Spike's sister Joie (who has acted in many of his films) and brother Cinque had written a screenplay about a family in Brooklyn in the 1970s. When they showed it to their more famous brother, he was intrigued. He helped them rewrite it and agreed to direct it. *Crooklyn* was unusual for Lee in that it was in no way provocative. Many reviewers felt that telling a more intimate story gave Lee the room to create more complex, realistic characters than he had in his other films.

The Lees claimed that very little of the story was actually autobiographical, but much of it did bear a striking resemblance to their own childhood. *Crooklyn*, their affectionate name for Brooklyn, concerned a family with a jazz musician father, a teacher mother, and five children.

Although, as in Lee's own family, the mother dies of cancer, much of the film consists of the children laughing and fighting and playing. Many of the events came directly from childhood recollections, such as the kids arguing over what to watch on television. Troy, the only girl in the family, loved *The Partridge Family*, while her oldest brother—like Spike—wanted to watch basketball. In another scene that closely mirrors Spike's childhood, the oldest son goes to an important Knicks game instead of to a concert where his father is performing his own compositions.

As an adult, Spike has remained passionately devoted to basketball. He owns a pair of courtside season tickets to the Knicks at Madison Square Garden. Although other celebrities show up for important games, none is such a big—or vocal—fan as Spike. He is there without fail, jumping up and down, yelling and cheering.

Spike works on the set of Crooklyn.

Sometimes this brings him more attention than he would like. During a playoff series against the Indiana Pacers in 1994, Lee began laying into Pacer guard Reggie Miller. Instead of throwing Miller off his game, Lee's taunts fired him up. Miller began dropping three-pointer after three-pointer. After each basket, he gestured toward Spike. Spike was on his feet, screaming for the Knicks to get on Miller. He had become part of the game. He and Miller kept yelling and gesturing at each other. Miller ended up scoring twenty-five points in the fourth quarter, and Indiana waltzed away with the game.

The next day, Spike was on the cover of every tabloid in New York City. "Thanks a lot Spike!" screamed the headline of the *New York Daily News*. It seemed everybody was blaming him for the Knicks' loss. "Sometimes he opens his mouth a little too much and gets the other guys going. Tonight was one of those nights," Miller said. Luckily for Spike, the Knicks came back to take the series. If they hadn't, "it would have been a long summer," he said later.

"Thanks a lot Spike!"

To Spike, he's just being a fan and just being himself. In 1997, he published *Best Seat in the House: A Basketball Memoir*, a book chronicling his life as a Knicks fan.

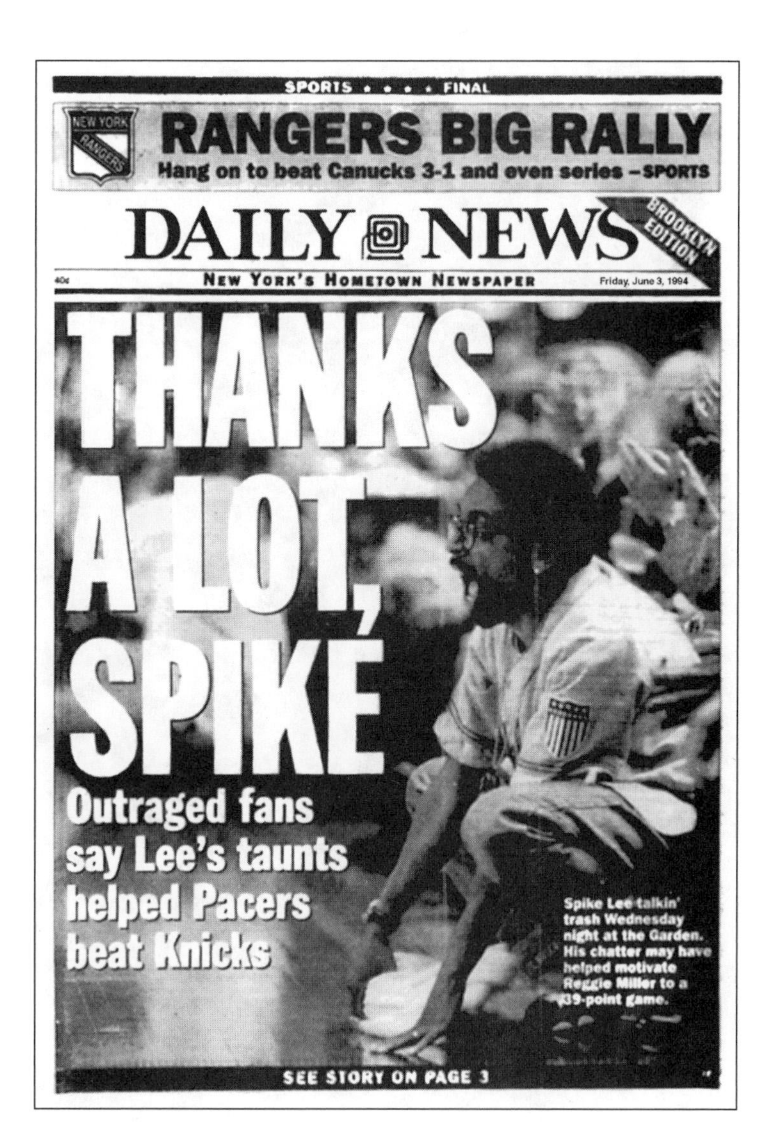

SPORTS • • • • FINAL

NEW YORK RANGERS

RANGERS BIG RALLY

Hang on to beat Canucks 3-1 and even series –SPORTS

DAILY NEWS

BROOKLYN EDITION

40¢ NEW YORK'S HOMETOWN NEWSPAPER Friday, June 3, 1994

THANKS A LOT, SPIKE

Outraged fans say Lee's taunts helped Pacers beat Knicks

Spike Lee talkin' trash Wednesday night at the Garden. His chatter may have helped motivate Reggie Miller to a 39-point game.

SEE STORY ON PAGE 3

During the 1994 playoffs, Spike became the subject of angry newspaper articles that claimed his yelling contributed to the Knicks' defeat.

Spike loves to cheer for the Knicks.

In recent years, Spike has continued to spread his wings as a filmmaker, trying new things and touching on different subjects. In 1995, he filmed and released *Clockers*, the story of a young drug dealer from a rough Brooklyn neighborhood. In the film, Lee tried to show the human side of a kid in trouble.

The following year, Lee made *Get on the Bus*, a film about a group of black men going to the Million-Man March in Washington, D.C. With this film, Lee again proved that there is more than one way to get a movie made. The film was funded entirely by private contributions from African-Americans. Each man in the film seems to represent a different aspect of African-American life, and as they travel cross-country from Los Angeles, they argue and talk, learning about themselves and the diverse elements of the black community. "A sermon wrapped in a road movie," *Newsweek* critic David Ansen called it. "At its best it can stir the soul."

Lee has also delved into the world of documentaries. In 1997, he made *4 Little Girls*, a film about four black children who were killed when a church in Birmingham, Alabama, was bombed in 1963, during the civil rights movement. He has also made a short documentary about Georgetown University basketball coach John Thompson for HBO's "Real Sports" program.

For his documentary 4 Little Girls, *Spike interviewed several people who were involved in the incident.*

Although none of Lee's recent films have captured the public's imagination the way that *Malcolm X* or *Do the Right Thing* did, he has continued to learn and grow as a filmmaker. New projects, such as *He Got Game*, starring Denzel Washington as the father of a top high school basketball player who must choose between going to college and turning pro, seem likely to catapult him back into the headlines.

A great businessman, Spike is involved in all kinds of endeavors. He always wanted millions of people to see his films, but he never thought the studios would be willing to spend enough money publicizing them. So early on, he hit on the idea of selling T-shirts and caps to promote his movies. It was a cheap, profitable, and efficient way of getting the word out. "Marketing is something I'm very proud of—the only person who does marketing better than me, as far as artists go, is Madonna. She's the champ," he once remarked. In 1990, he opened a store in his old Brooklyn neighborhood called Spike's Joint, which sells merchandise promoting his movies.

"Marketing is something I'm very proud of."

He has other business enterprises, as well. In addition to 40 Acres and a Mule Filmworks, his film production company, Spike has his own

A talented promoter and businessman, Spike has opened a store of his own in Brooklyn.

record label, 40 Acres and a Mule Musicworks. He has been making commercials since the very beginning of his career, most famously for Nike, but also for products such as Levi's and Diet Coke.

In 1996, Spike proved his commitment to working in advertising by forming his own agency, Spike DDB, in association with DDB Needham Worldwide, one of the industry leaders. Some people are amazed that he has the energy for all these different ventures. To Spike, it's all just business. "I don't think I'm doing anything different from anyone else able to get opportunities and parlay them into business enterprises," he says. "I'm not going to limit myself to feature films."

Many people believe that Spike's greatest talent is as a businessman. Revered actor Ossie Davis, who has appeared in many of Lee's films, says, "Spike has the temperament and sensibility and drive of the founding fathers of Hollywood—the Samuel Goldwyns and Louis B. Mayers. They were geniuses at marketing. I admire Spike as a writer, although he has a long way to go. I admire him as a director and as an actor. But it is as a mass marketer that Spike is a genius. This is what black people need in America—to learn how to

"Spike is where black Americans need to go. Spike is American to the core."

integrate their power with the power structure. Spike is where black Americans need to go. Spike is American to the core."

Spike Lee has opened the door for many young black people to get into filmmaking. He tries to employ as many African-Americans as possible on his film crews, giving them a chance where other people might not.

He also led the way for a generation of black directors, such as John Singleton and Albert and Allan Hughes, who have produced searing films about inner-city violence. When Spike first came on the scene, Hollywood was producing virtually no films by black directors. Today, a dozen are often released in a single year.

Spike has tried to ensure that this stream will continue by educating people about how films are made. He has taught film classes at Harvard University and Long Island University and has written books about how he made his own films. "I hope to further demystify the filmmaking process," Spike wrote in his book about *Do the Right Thing*. "Film is no hocus-pocus magic stuff. That's what Hollywood wants you to believe so you don't attempt to tell your own stories."

Telling his own stories is what Spike does best. In the coming years, he will undoubtedly continue to make movies that provoke and entertain Americans of all races. He will put flesh-and-blood characters on the screen—lively, funny, and sometimes aggravating characters who challenge us to look honestly in the mirror and at the world. Whatever projects Spike chooses to pursue, one thing is certain: He will do so on his own terms.

Spike is eager to pass on his knowledge of filmmaking to younger students. Here he lectures at Harvard.

CHRONOLOGY

1957	March 20: Spike is born in Atlanta, Georgia.
1960s & 1970s	Spike's father moves the family to New York City; Spike grows up in Brooklyn.
1975	Spike graduates from high school and attends Morehouse College in Atlanta.
1977	Spike takes moving pictures of block dancing and the Great Blackout in New York City. Later, he combines the images into a documentary: *Last Hustle in Brooklyn*.
1979	Spike graduates from Morehouse and decides on a career in film. He enters New York University Film School in the fall.
1983	Spike finishes *Joe's Bed-Stuy Barbershop: We Cut Heads*. The film wins a student Academy Award.

1986	Spike completes *She's Gotta Have It*, which becomes the most successful independent film of its time.
1988	Recounting his time at Morehouse College, Spike makes *School Daze*, a film that explores differences among African-Americans.
1989	Spike makes *Do the Right Thing*, a film that investigates race in America. The film generates tremendous controversy and debate throughout the country.
1990	In *Mo' Better Blues*, his next film, Spike looks at the musical art of jazz. Spike also opens a store in his old Brooklyn neighborhood called Spike's Joint.
1991	Spike tells the story of a romantic relationship between a black man and a white woman in *Jungle Fever*.
1992	In his most ambitious and controversial project, Spike tells the story of Malcolm X, a black nationalist who became an important leader in the 1950s and 1960s.
1993	Spike marries Tonya Lewis.
1994	Spike is criticized in the press after his trash-talking inspires Reggie Miller to help the Indiana Pacers defeat the New York Knicks in a playoff game.

1996	Spike makes a documentary called *4 Little Girls*, about a bomb that exploded in a black church in Birmingham, Alabama.
1997	Spike makes *Get on the Bus*, a film about the Million-Man March.
1998	Spike's most recent film, *He Got Game*, is about one of his favorite subjects: basketball.

GLOSSARY

cinematographer a person who shoots the camera for a movie production

clique a small group of people that stay to themselves and won't interact with others

gig an entertainer or musician's job to play a show or several shows

independent film a movie made without the money, or influence, of major studios in Hollywood, California

internship an unpaid position where a person gets the opportunity to learn about a career

liberal a person who is open minded

pilgrimage a journey to a sacred place, usually religious

screening a special presentation of a movie

tabloid a type of newspaper that uses exciting and sensational headlines and stories to attract readers

tuition the price to take classes at a school

A NOTE ON SOURCES

Although no thorough adult biography has been written about Spike Lee, James Earl Hardy's *Spike Lee: Filmmaker* (New York: Chelsea House, 1996), a young adult book, provides an excellent overview of his life and career. Spike Lee himself has written a number of books about the making of his movies, which offer an inside glimpse at Lee and the filmmaking process. These books often include diaries he kept while shooting and insightful comments from other people who worked on the films. Among the most useful of these are *Spike Lee's Gotta Have It: Inside Guerrilla Filmmaking* (New York: Fireside, 1987), *Do the Right Thing* (New York: Fireside, 1989), which he wrote with Lisa Jones, and *By Any Means Necessary: The Trials and Tribulations of the Making of Malcolm X* (New York: Hyperion, 1992), which he wrote with Ralph Wiley. Lee and Wiley also collaborated on *Best Seat in the House: A Basketball*

Memoir (New York: Crown, 1997), which interweaves the events in Lee's life with a discussion of the changes in professional basketball during the last thirty years. It has more information about Lee's childhood than is available elsewhere.

Another great resource for information about Spike Lee is the New York Public Library for the Performing Arts, which has files of newspaper and magazine articles about Lee, along with collections of movie reviews. Of course, there is no way to really know Spike Lee without seeing his movies, which are available in most video stores and many libraries throughout the country.

FOR MORE INFORMATION

BOOKS

Hardy, James Earl. *Spike Lee: Filmmaker*. New York: Chelsea House, 1996.

Haskings, Jim. *Spike Lee: By Any Means Necessary*. New York: Walker and Company, 1997.

Lee, Spike. *Spike Lee's Gotta Have It: Inside Guerrilla Filmmaking*. New York: Fireside, 1987.

Lee, Spike, with Lisa Jones. *Do the Right Thing*. New York: Fireside, 1989.

Lee, Spike, with Ralph Wiley. *Best Seat in the House: A Basketball Memoir.* New York: Crown, 1997.

INTERNET SITES

http:\\www.40acres.com
This is the home page of Spike Lee's production company, 40 Acres and a Mule.

http:\\www.celebsite.com\people\spikelee
This site has biographical information and connections to other websites.

http:\\www.hotwired.com\popfeatures\96\23\lee.guide.html
In addition to biographical information, this site contains an array of quotes by and about Lee and connections to other websites.

http:\\www.voyagerco.com\movies\directors\spike
This site contains a complete listing of everything Lee has done, including commercials, music videos, student films, and books.

INDEX

ABOUT THE AUTHOR

Melissa McDaniel is a writer and editor living in New York City. *Spike Lee* is her first book for Franklin Watts. Her second book for Franklin Watts, *W.E.B. DuBois*, will be published in 1999.